ME

&

MRS

JONES

ME
&
MRS
JONES

JUSTINE GLADDEN

atmosphere press

ON
THE
ROAD

Every two to three weeks, the sales team would move to another city or town or state. Loading into a couple of vans, we would ride caravan-style to the next stop. Between stops for gas, food, and bathroom breaks, we would sing, listen to music, and tell jokes.

We were selling magazines and books, fashion, sports, health, Bibles, Cookbooks, dictionaries, general news, etc.—for large companies. Every salesperson had a daily quota to meet, either for sales or production, and we were always trying to beat ourselves. If one day you hit 100 sales, naturally the next day you shoot for higher. You were always shooting for that "highest day" and that number always kept growing.

POSITIONS ON THE JOB

The field supervisors, known as the car handlers, were the people who actually drove our big fifteen-passenger van and determined the neighborhoods and areas we would be working in that day. We called these "territories." The handler would pick out the territory according to the person. Some people liked working in what we call "power territory," which is a town with the biggest houses like hotels. Some people, however, liked to work in what we call "sales territory." This category included smaller houses or apartments where there were more people. A higher volume of people in a given area often generated more sales. Some people liked to work businesses and land those large subscriptions. Businesses could be big spenders because what they bought was often a tax write-off so they could spend as much as they wanted through a business account. Every salesperson had their own cup of tea. when it came to preferable sales territories. A good field supervisor knew where to put everybody on a daily basis. A good car handler always looked out for their sales crew.

The office manager was the person who took care of the payroll, reservations for the hotels, and all of the pertinent bookkeeping for the sales team. They would also get everybody what they call "drawer money" for that evening for dinner and breakfast. I held that position for several years and became office manager for my own group. To be a good office manager, it is not only very important to know the ins and outs of the magazine-selling business, but it is also good to be extremely trustworthy because you were dealing with all of the funds to make sure everybody got paid.

The ad runner, however, was one of the most important roles in the business. The ad runner generated the people. I was considered one of the best ad runners because I would hire people from a newspaper or radio ad or hire people right out of the neighborhoods where we sold magazines. I would make up flyers, go where everybody hung out, and distribute them in the pool halls, clubs, beauty and barbershops, and basketball courts. I would even put them in mailboxes and people would call me up. I would do a pre-screening on the phone and ask them their age and how free they were to travel, then I would set them up for an interview. If I hired them, I would give them a time to start, have them pack their clothes, and go to the local bus station. I had an account with Greyhound where I would order them a ticket, they would get on the bus, and I would send them to whichever state or city the crew was in. I would call ahead to let the secretary know they were coming and what time they would arrive, and somebody would be there to pick them up at the bus station. I broke records on hiring people. I was known as what they called a "double-barrel shotgun" because if the ad or the radio didn't pop, I would go hit the streets and hire people. I've met and hired all kinds of people. I got a reputation for being one of the baddest ad runners in the company because I was able to talk total strangers into packing all that they own, saying goodbye to their families, and leaving with someone they didn't even know to travel and sell magazines door-to-door.

When a person wants you to have a good day, instead of saying break a leg, in the magazine business we would say *get a bunch*. What we meant was to get a bunch of sales. We also said *ditto* a lot.

New people are the lifeline of the business, so another saying means that, for us to continue to grow and get bigger, better, and stronger, we have to continue to bring in new people, both recruiters and employees. The more we bring in, the better, because the better we grow as a whole.

STRICTORECTAMITUS

This is a word we came up with that means when the cords in your eyes get crossed up with the cords in your ass, you have a shitty outlook on life. So when somebody is really negative, has a bad attitude, isn't doing well, talks about quitting and going home, or just doesn't want to be there anymore, we say they have strictorectamitis.

Are you free to travel or do you want to travel free? is what we ask to let people know that the job is designed for you to be able to be free to travel, learn the job, make money, and cover your own expenses. So we say to make sure they understand with the position that it is about being able to be free to travel and not traveling for free because if you want to travel free then you had the wrong place. There's no such thing as traveling for free—you have to pay your way through the sales of books and magazines.

If you are in this business for any length of time and you can't figure out how to get a sale or convince "Mrs. Jones" to buy something from you, then you need to go to your room and practice. You can't have fun and party and not do what you were hired to do. You have to know the job and you have to do the job.

For example, this was my sales conversation—First, I would knock on the door, and when they came to the door I would say:

Hi, my name is Justine. I'm with an on-the-job training program being sponsored by _____. Have you read or heard anything about it? No? Great, then I'll be the first one to explain it to you and get you to back me up as well. By the way, who do I have the pleasure of speaking with? Pleased to meet you. This on-the-job training program is designed to teach, train, and motivate young adults like myself to come out and talk to people in the community. How am I doing so far? Great! Then, so that we don't have to ask you for a donation or charity, they gave us a tool to work with and that tool is selling books and magazine subscriptions. All your neighbors have been picking out any three, five, or seven of their favorite publications. This allows me credit points to earn a cash award. I am working to win $1000 and I can only get that through the points from the sales of the books and magazines. So which three, five, or seven can I count you in for?

That was basically the sales talk. Pretty much everything after that was a conversation in selling myself and my personality and getting the person to like me enough to invest in my future. That's basically what you were doing—getting "Mr." or "Mrs. Jones" to like you enough to invest in your future. It didn't make a difference what you were selling...books, magazines, pencils, toothpicks—if they liked you, they were going to buy whatever it is you were selling.

QUOTATUDE

This is the attitude when you have your quota then your attitude is a lot better. You're smiling, you have a positive outlook on life, you even talk to people differently. So we say *quotatude,* which means the mood that you are in because you met your quota.

THE *PUMP IT UP* SONG

Every morning, to get ready for the day, we sang. We have songs that we sing. We have positive quotes. We have positive thoughts for the day and we also announce the activities of the day. So the *get ready* song is a segment that several people on the crew would make up with a rhyming tune and sing in the morning meeting when their name was called. For instance, the *get ready* song that I had was, "Good morning crew!" They would say, "Aha aha." I would say, "How you do?" They would say, "Aha aha." I would say, "You're rolling with the TNT crew." They would say, "Aha aha." I would say, "So now you know what I'm about, I got one more thing to freak you out! My name is Tina and I'm not so meana but the totals that I run will make you screama. So now you know what I'm about and I'm going to let someone freak you out!" Then the next person would come in with their song. We had one song that went "Good morning crew, how do you do? You know I'm rolling with that number one crew. So now you know what I'm about. I got one more thing to freak you out, on Tee! I don't be joking. I find a Jones like a Newport and I smoke them and when I drop that receipt, yes I choked them. So now you know what I'm about and I'm going to let someone else freak you out." We had several of these songs and I would add more as I went on.

MASTER
OF
YOUR
EMOTIONS

This is what we would say to convey that you are in control of your own destiny. You are in control of your own situation. Whatever happens to you is because of you. You control your attitude and the way you feel. The way you see life, the way you think—it's all on you, so master that and control your emotions.

WAB

When someone called you a WAB, it meant you were weak and boring (to be nice about it) or a weak-ass bitch or bastard. It meant that you could not do the job and you were weak, but you had nothing else to do or nowhere else to go so you stayed. WAB is the lowest of insults in our company.

MR.
AND
MRS.
JONES

When we were in our territories, we would go door to door. Because we did not know the names of the people who lived there, we would call them "Mr. and Mrs. Jones." So we would ask Mrs. Jones to pick out any three,five, or seven of her favorite magazines and that's how we got our points to earn our cash rewards or vacations. The more magazines they picked, the bigger the order would be and the more commission and points we would make. We had a case that held the receipts, the magazine list, and the price cards. Our identification and a pen to write with we called it a ducket because everything we needed was inside of it we would love to drop somebody full term because the longer the term the more the order. if somebody took one magazine for one year it would be a certain price but if they took it for 3 years it would be more so the more terms the more money so we had a saying drop them at full term if you could.

Once, on a nice sunny day in Vallejo, California, I was feeling really good about myself. I was working on having a high day but it just seemed like the air was not right, almost like the calm before the storm. I was positive anyway. If I'm not mistaken, I was in a neighborhood of nice, beautiful homes. We called it "power territory" because the houses were really beautiful, so I knew I was going to have me a dropper. I knocked on the door and then waited for about two seconds and knocked again. There were two cars in the driveway. About a second later, the door opened and there was a gun pointed at my face. I backed up and said, "Whoa ma'am! I'm just selling books and magazines trying to earn a living! I'm selling books and magazines to better myself!" She put the gun down and said, "I'm so sorry, this lady was messing with my husband. We just finished arguing on the phone and she said she was coming to get his clothes. I thought you were her."

I stood there frozen for a minute. I was shaking like a leaf but, even though I was scared to death, I didn't feel bad. I assumed this was going to be my day but she was so apologetic that she invited me into the house and asked me what I was doing. I told her. She bought $500 worth of magazines and offered to cook me dinner. She was a really nice lady who was just in a bad situation, so I hurried to get my stuff together and got out of there before the other lady got there because I didn't want to be involved in any shootings.

THE CREDENTIAL

The credential was a list that we would show Mrs. Jones. It had our name, the company's name, a description of us—height, weight, hair color, eye color—and what we were working for...20,000 credit points to earn a $1,000 cash reward. We would show Mrs. Jones the front page of what we were working for along with our ID, and then put it in her hand so we could hold a receipt, the ducket, and a pen to write them up. We would turn the pages and show them which magazines we had to offer. Some magazines were on the even split list, which we got more points for than the off split list, so of course we pushed the even split list the most. After they picked from the list, they would have to sign their name and leave a comment about what they thought about our presentation and how many points they allowed us. It was called a personal point rating sheet. Then we would fold it back up and go to the next door.

We would have yearly competitions similar to a Mr. or Mrs. America contest. We did a talent portion, bathing suit modeling, and a formal outfit. They picked the top salespeople in the company to compete. They would give out trophies for who had the most sales for the year, the most production for the year, the most quoted days, or who was the best trainer, and so on. I won the contest two years in a row, skipped one year, and won it again for a total of three champion years. They had a bulletin that came out every month that kept up with everybody's sales score and production so you could keep up with people in different groups to see who was doing what. You could win trips to Hawaii or Jamaica, or you could take the money, and we always hollered, "Take the money!" It was very competitive and a lot of fun.

DROPS

We called each period of the day a *drop*. We normally had three to four drops per day. The first drop in the morning was for two to two and a half hours. The second drop was two and a half hours. The third drop was two and a half hours, sometimes three, and the fourth drop would just be to get out and grab a sale or two and get back in while they were picking everybody else up. Some people would have stronger first drops than second drops, and some people would have better evening drops than they had morning drops because more people were home in the evening.

COMEBACKS

Comebacks are something that we used to change the Jones' minds if they said no or were not interested. We had a comeback for each objection. So if they said they were not interested, we would say, "I don't blame you. I wouldn't be interested in nothing I didn't know about either, so let me tell you what I'm doing." And they would say, "Could you come back tomorrow?" Then we would come back with, "But tomorrow is not promised to us, so don't put off tomorrow something you can do today." Then Mrs. Jones would say, "My husband has the checkbook." We said, "That's okay, most of the customers were paying in cash today and I have change if you need it." So every time they made an excuse about why they could not buy, we had a comeback for why they should buy.

AN
OLD
HEAD

An old head is a person who's been in the business more than a year. They would teach, train, and motivate other young people about the ins and outs of the business. They held meetings, made room checks, and offered shirts and ties to the new people.

THE
HOTELS

The hotels that we lived in when we traveled state-to-state were very nice. We would work to have the hotels we stay in for two to three weeks. We would have them take out the beds of one or two rooms to use as an office. We put up our computers and file cabinets and tables where people would come in and check in at night. We also made sure they had a meeting room where we could hold our sales meetings in the mornings and motivational *Pump It Up* meetings. We tried to stay close to restaurants where salespeople could go eat at night and find convenience stores close by. Each hotel we went to, we stayed two to three weeks and the hotels were pretty familiar with us so they knew to keep us all together so we would only disturb each other and not any other guests. Most rooms had two to three salespeople rooming together. There were couples that had their own rooms but they were salespeople that had been there longer and were making enough money to afford the rent split two ways. Then we had people occupying single rooms by themselves, but they were paying for it themselves. When you first came in as a new person, you had to sleep two to three to a room. So if it was three guys, whoever had the most sales for that day would get the bed and it would rotate, giving everybody a chance to have the bed. It was an *Old Head* who kept the bed by themselves because they wrote the most sales. The other two slept head to toe in the other bed.

THE FLOWERS I SENT

While I was on the road, I would talk to my daughter periodically just to see how she was doing. I would send flowers to the house, school, or wherever she was at that particular time. That was my way of mothering from a distance and letting her know that I was thinking about her and everything was okay. Not only did she love the flowers but it made her day and made the problem a little easier to deal with. If it was a boyfriend that she was having a problem with he would think some other guy liked her and was sending her flowers—that always seemed to make things better for her, so I spent a lot of money sending flowers over the years. I also sent candy baskets and fruit baskets. I even had dancing clowns go to the school until they made a rule that I couldn't because of the kids getting jealous. But I used to love to send flowers and candy and balloons and fruit baskets to the school to let her know that I was always thinking about her and that she was very special and important to me.

HIRING
NEW
PEOPLE

When I was knocking on doors in the neighborhoods where there were African-American people, if I saw a teenage daughter or son in the house I would ask them if they needed a job. If they said yes, I would tell them to pack their clothes to last for a couple days and I would be standing on my pickup with a new girl or guy. I realized that I could hire people that way and that, instead of knocking on doors and being a salesperson, I could sell people on joining the company. Over time, I got better and better to where the supervisor decided to take me off territory and make me the recruiter. He would place ads in the newspaper or on the radio in different towns and cities and I would go there to find a hotel with a meeting room. When people called from the radio ads or the newspaper, I would set them up for an interview in the hotel and explain all about the job. If they sounded interested, I would tell them to go home, pack their stuff, and meet me back at the hotel to start training. I did that for a long time at a very high volume and became good at it, but over a period of time certain towns and cities wouldn't get a large response from the ads so I decided to go into the neighborhoods. I made flyers to pass out, put them in the mailbox or at their door, or just handed them to people walking down the street. I would say, "Hey, looking for a job? Call this number. They're hiring people right now to start work tomorrow." I became the number one recruiter for the company. There are people in the business twenty years later that still credit me for hiring them from just walking down the street or riding a bicycle or catching them at a store. They said if I had not given them that flyer, they never would have had the opportunity to do the job that they were doing and that's how I hired new people.

BABIES ON BOARD

Can you imagine how many pregnancies happened on the crew in ten or fifteen years? I can recall it seeming like every month that somebody got pregnant because there was so much mixing and mismatching of new people coming and going, relationships starting and ending—there was so much going on. If a woman on the crew wanted to have the baby, she would have to go home and get off the road because we couldn't have babies on the road. Who would take care of them? So then the guy who got her pregnant would tell the girl that she would have to get an abortion if she wanted to stay. So all of a sudden the girl in the meeting did not get in the van and the next day she was sick in bed and after all of that they would wind up breaking up anyway and then he'd get somebody else pregnant and so on and so forth. It kept going on and on and on. I would not have wanted to be the person to talk the guy into telling the girl to get an abortion. To have all those babies on me, I wouldn't be able to breathe or think right now. But that's how it went when you lived on the road—certain sacrifices had to be made because most of the females wanted to stay there and be with the man who got her pregnant so they had to make a choice it was either the man and staying there hoping to keep him or go home and have your baby thinking that he's going to be with you then and it was some females that did that but never seen the man again and wind up raising the child by themselves anyway so that was the choices you had. I know some of those girls would give anything to turn back time and make a different decision—maybe not to keep the baby, but to take a different way of doing it. I was one of those girls. I think back on what it could have been: a girl or a boy and where would they be in my life now.

THE WOMEN'S CLUB

We had about ten to fifteen women on the crew that had been there over three years. They were considered *old heads* and we would try to come up with ideas to keep the crew motivated and upbeat, especially around the holidays when they were away from home and their families. We would come up with talent shows. The *Mr. and Mrs. Contest,* prizes, win trips, entertainment, beauty spa, and all kinds of things just to keep us motivated. We came up with a club and we called it the Women's Club. Which stands for (We Open Many Eyes Now). To be in the Women's Club, you had to have been there at least three years, had a high day over 200, a high week over 1000, and a great attitude.

We had a president, vice president, secretary, and treasurer. We also took dues of $5 a week. That money went into a savings account, and at the end of year we would use it to take a trip. One year it was Jamaica, another year Hawaii, and we would plan different trips each year according to how much money we raised. At first, we started out with the contest at the holidays and then turned it into a daily thing where we would sell coffee, donuts, hot chocolate, and sometimes biscuits in the morning meetings. We also opened up the Woman's Club store, one of the hotel rooms where we would sell chips, drinks, cigarettes, and other stuff that the crew might want. We would buy in bulk from Sam's Club and sell it to the crew. We traveled almost 100 to 150 people strong, which was a nice little organization. Sometimes on Wednesday nights we made chili and hot dogs and on the weekend. Just little stuff to make extra money—and that we did. With the money, we went on trips. It was like "what happens in Vegas stays in Vegas" where nobody knew exactly what happened on these trips except for the Woman's Club. We had some wild parties—I mean all night long, drinking, partying, smoking, just having a good time. We had strippers come in and dance for us. We had guys come in and give us massages and body wraps. We got our hair and nails done and just had a good time, treating ourselves after working all year round with the crew. It was fun and we became closer as a unit by being in the Woman's Club. It was almost like a sorority; we kept each other's business, we only talked amongst each other on certain issues, and there was a code of ethics that you had to go by to be a part of the Woman's Club. We didn't gossip or fight—if we had an attitude or problem, we'd all get together and figure it out amongst ourselves and that's kind of what kept us going as a unit. It also kept morale up with the company because everybody that came into the business wanted to be in the Woman's Club. We were an elite organization.

I remember one time we went to Jamaica and were playing games in the hotel room, just having fun and revealing unexpected secrets that stayed right in that room. and kind of made us look at some of the women funny because some things you just never assumed. I knew that they would say or do anything, we also found out about some of the women in the women's club liked the women in the women's club a little bit more than normal and we would wonder how sometimes some of the women would disappear and we wouldn't see them for a couple hours and then they would come back like nothing happened so because we were a team we asked no questions we did not want to know the answers to but it was all good to each his own if they didn't bother me I didn't bother them. When we got back to the crew nothing else was said.

There were also several people in the organization that wanted to do things to add to the crew: the guys wanted to start a men's club, new people wanted to start a new people's club, and so on and so forth. There were women on the crew that could cook and had their own little restaurant thing going. They would come in, in the evening, cook a nice meal, and sell plates to people who wanted a home-cooked meal and didn't feel like going to a restaurant. There were other people who pressed clothes and would iron the crew's clothes so they could look good out on territory every day. We also ran our own beauty shop and barbershop. We had a cleaners we called it and some people would buy clothes on sale and sell them to people in the organization. Some guys would buy alcohol and sell drinks or shots in the evening. We had all these businesses running inside of a business.

QUOTA WEEK BY SATURDAY

Everybody on the crew had a quota. It was designed to keep things equal and fair among the people on the crew according to the length of time they were there, so as a new person your quota would be five sales for $50. As time went on and you wrote more business, your quota got higher and higher—so if your quota was ten sales for $100, then working six days a week put your weekly quota at sixty sales for $600. Most of the top agents' quotas were ten sales for $200, so their weekly total would have been sixty sales for $1200. And if you worked really hard and met your quota by Friday, you could take Saturday off or go for more sales to earn more money and win more bonuses.

But I wanted to know what management was doing in the hotel on Saturdays so I would work really hard to meet my weekly quota by Friday so I could take Saturday off. I would wait until the crew left and then hovered around the hotel rooms to see what was going on. I did this quite often to the manager/owner of the company. Seeing that I was being nosy and wanted to get in on the action, So they said "You might as well let her in 'cause she's gonna take off Every Saturday so that she can hang around us and see what's going on." I found out management was partying, getting high, doing all kinds of stuff—and I wanted to be a part of it.

THE
CREW
KIDS

The *crew kids* were the children of the salespeople. People with children would have them come out in the summertime or over holidays when they were out of school. The crew kids knew pretty much everything there was to know about door-to-door sales because they stayed with their parents for long periods of time on the job. They stayed in the hotel pool all day, they ate at restaurants, and we had a nanny that took care of the kids during the day. We all chipped in and paid her to take care of the kids. She would also teach them reading, writing, and swimming, and took them out to eat and. It all depended on how old they were, but some of the fifteen- and sixteen-year-olds would go out on drops and knock on doors to make money to buy their own school clothes. Some went to territory with their parents, which was an extra incentive for the parents because they could show The Joneses what they were working for. So Mr. and Mrs. Jones would buy big because they could see how the parent was trying to better themselves and their family.

MY MENTOR

I remember when I first saw my mentor, I thought he was a very nice-looking man but he had a woman. I had a man as well but he came into the organization as somebody who knew what they were doing. I paid attention to him but he handled other people on the crew and I had my own car handler so I really didn't get a chance to interact too much with him. Over time, my field supervisor was out for the day and he put me in the car with my soon-to-be mentor, Mr. Sito. That morning, I was ready to go out and have a hell of a day. They told me I would be riding with Mr. Sito and I automatically felt pessimistic because I was so used to riding with my other field supervisor. I didn't want to back up nobody's else's action and make nobody else money but him but I had no choice. While we were on our way to that day's territory, he started asking questions like what our favorite territories and what type of tea we liked, and what type of areas we were used to working. I told him that I liked working in what we called "Black territory."

My people are everything and all I wanted was in the Black territory...the soul food. I would eat lunch there, would sell to business owners and other customers. I would sell to everybody that came into the bar or pool room or barbershop. I got a chance to meet some guys in the territory, too, so Black territory was my cup of tea. Customers paid in cash so I knew the orders were good.

Sometimes I would stay in the same territory the whole time we were in town and go right back to the same place I left off. Everybody knew me so that was the best place to be. I would go into a bar between orders and shoot some pool, meeting friends, dancing, and having a good time. But as he spotted everybody out in their territory, he told me to go into an area that I wasn't familiar with. I wasn't getting out so I told him I didn't work in this kind of territory and he said he didn't have time to take me to my tea so I had to work it today. I told him no, that's not how it goes, so we got into an argument and he decided he was going to make me get out of the car in that territory. I refused to get out of the van. He tried to pull me out of the van. We hustled back and forth until Mrs. Jones saw us struggling in the van and decided to call the police because she thought I was being attacked and he was trying to kidnap me. The police came and immediately grabbed him, threw him up against the car, put handcuffs on him, and took him to jail. Another officer grabbed me, put me in the car, and took me down to the precinct to press charges. On the way there I was thinking, *this is going to be really bad when I get back to the hotel tonight.* I called the manager there and told her what had happened and she told me to drop the charges. I told her he attacked me. He tried to pull me out of the van. She still said drop the charges, so I dropped the charges.

While I was sitting waiting for them to release him, I was scared, knowing I had to get back in the van with this man to go back to the hotel. I thought he was going to try to kill me because I wouldn't get out of the car and caused his arrest, but he came out and walked right past me. I went on behind him and he didn't say one word all the way back to the hotel. I did not get back in the van with him anymore. because of this situation, but I guess time has a way of healing things because we eventually started speaking. After that, I got pregnant by my boyfriend and got off the road so I could have my baby.

My boyfriend at that time sent me to his mother's house to have the baby. While I was there, I guess he got lonely and started messing with one of the girls on the crew. I would call him at 9 or 10 o'clock at night and some female would answer the phone. I would ask him who it was and he would hang up the phone. I decided I didn't want to be at his mother's house anymore since he was cheating on me. I decided to go home to my mother's house so. I went home, had my baby, and when I got ready to get back on the road, the owner of the company suggested that I go to Mr. Sito's crew because he was a new manager. I thought, "Oh no, he's going to pay me back for what I did to him" and I was so scared and nervous. I didn't want to go back to the crew where my boyfriend was because I would have to look at them in their faces. By that time he was seeing another woman and they were a couple. I decided I didn't want to deal with that, so I went to Mr. Sito's crew. And as they say, the rest is history because he did not make me feel any other way than welcome. I came in and he introduced me to everybody as a person with a lot of experience. He spoke highly of me and really made me feel welcome so I figured to let bygones be bygones and forget about the past. I was trying to impress him to show him that there were no hard feelings.

I remember I left the crew one time to go home, following a boyfriend who wanted me to prove my love.

Mr. Sito came driving through my town, saying he was passing through. I don't know how he was doing that because we were 400 miles off his path, but he came through just to check on me and see how I was doing. I'll never forget that because I was kind of down and out, depressed going through some stuff with my boyfriend. He wasn't who he was supposed to be or treating me like I should have been treated and I was getting pretty fed up at that point. And then here comes Mr. Sito driving through. He said, "How are you doing? Just wanted to check on you, make sure you're okay and see if you needed anything, and to let you know that I'm always here no matter what." That meant a lot to me because nobody had ever said that to me in my life. No family member, no relative—nobody had ever told me that they would be there for me no matter what. So it was then I really fell in love with him. Of course, I went back on the road and it seemed like nothing had changed. We were still the same people: friends; he was still my surrogate man—anything I needed, whether physical, personal, or spiritual. I could talk to him about my family. I didn't want for anything because of him, so I was there for him too. He trusted me so much that he promoted me to office manager, which allowed me to do payroll. I handled all his money. I checked in with him at night and gave him all his money. He paid me on the weekend and we never had a discrepancy about a dime, so I consider this man a mentor because he was there for all phases of my life.

I remember he was going through a little situation and I was there for him. He would call me and I would come running no matter what. He knew that he could count on me in a time of distress and I was there because he was there for me. But as time went on, life went on, and I met someone. I married them and got off the road for a little while because it's hard having a relationship on the road with so many distractions. I thought it would be good if I concentrated on my marriage and got off the road to try to live a different way. Mr. Sito and I still communicated with each other. Every time he came through town we would have lunch and spend time together. Until one day I got a call to tell me that he had passed away. My heart dropped to the floor. I just felt like everything I knew and everything I felt about this person was gone. He was so important to me. I still miss his presence and wish that I could just speak with him one more time. It's very rare to find people you feel this way about, but he was one of them and I have never met anyone else like him. I decided to write this book and to dedicate it to him as my mentor and best friend.

DRESS CODE

The organization had a dress code. The girls could wear pretty much anything as long as it wasn't too short, too tight, or too revealing. They wore skorts, capris, and tennis shoes for comfort, or T-shirts, nice blouses, and bright colors to brighten up their face. The guys had to wear shirts and ties. They could wear jeans, sneakers, and shorts but had to have on a tie.

NOT WORKING ON TERRITORY

This would happen when a salesperson was negative, had an argument with somebody, didn't feel good, or were scared of or didn't like the territory. They would find things to do like go to a mall and walk around all day or sit in a restaurant and meet somebody. If they were working in a complex that had a pool, they would sit by the pool, take naps, or play cards. The managers were not so much bothered by the lack of sales but by how they would burn their territory up so nobody else could work it. If a person came through and saw a stranger on the corner for an hour or so, it looked suspicious. Now nobody else can go into the territory because they might get reported and picked up. It made things a lot worse because you didn't get paid and you drew attention to the crew.

THE
CREW
DRAMA

When I first joined the crew, I was rooming with this girl named Priscilla. She was going with one of the field supervisors. She was real bubbly and always had a great attitude. I remember we were on territory one day and she had a habit of always running out in the street, twirling around and dancing, especially if she had a good day. She would celebrate her sales victories. One day she was adding up her totals for the day and by the time we got to Main St., she realized it had been her highest day. She started dancing in the street and an eighteen-wheeler came along and hit her. I remember seeing her laying there with her face all scratched up and her eyes open, looking at things around her, still smiling because she was celebrating her high day. I guess when she got hit, the expression on her face never changed and that stayed with me because I had never seen anybody get killed before. It was very dramatic and I just hope her soul is resting in peace because she was a very sweet person.

We also had a friend who was doing drugs. We didn't know to what extent, but she had a good attitude and was always upbeat and we thought it was just her personality until we found out it was substance abuse. I remember we went to this town in California and she went and got drugs for everybody on the crew because she had a vehicle. They called her the runner. One night, she ran out to get some drugs and I guess she had run out of money and decided she was gonna snatch the drugs and run. She went down a street and when the dealer put the dope in her hand, she took off, not knowing it was a one-way street. She had to turn the car around and pass the drug dealers again and when she did they shot at her. I'm not sure what type of weapon it was but it was so horrible that when they had to go clean out the car there was so much blood they could hardly clean it out. They had to practically remove the seat covers and the floor rugs just to get most of the stuff out. She was a beautiful person and I never forget how she always told me to keep my head up and think positive. It was so sad because everybody really loved her and she wasn't a bad person or trying to do any harm to anyone. She just got caught up in the drugs.

Another one of the crew, a young man, was also doing drugs. It was really bad and the manager decided he wasn't going to take it anymore and let him run out and get drugs or get high. One night, someone came to the hotel to bring him drugs. A couple hours went by before the manager went into the young man's room and found the dope man in the room selling him drugs. He told the dope man to leave, that he didn't want any and he wasn't going to allow him to get high. The dope man stabbed the manager to death and sold the young man drugs anyway. So the manager gave up his life to save someone else's but it really didn't make a difference because the young man kept on getting high and never changed his life. Sometimes it does not pay to try to help someone because you wind up losing your life and they will still get high.

There was a young lady that was knocking on doors to get orders and it was getting dark. She noticed three guys were following her so she ran to the corner for her pick up. They ran behind her, grabbed her, pulled her into the woods, and raped her. I remember when she came back to the hotel that night, she had blood on the side of her face. I remember asking her who she beat up and she burst out crying saying that these three white guys jumped on her and raped her. She had called the police and they never came so she had come back to the hotel. She called the police again and they never came. She was scared and came back to the hotel. They filled out a report but because they were white guys and she was a black girl, they didn't do a lot about the situation and told her she could go down and file a report but that meant she would have to stay in town. She didn't know anybody and didn't have enough money to stay in town until the court date so she didn't press charges or pursue it and neither did the police but she was never the same again. From then on, when she went on territory, she wanted to work in the malls or areas that weren't secluded so she would feel safe.

Most of the managers in the organization were intelligent, hard-working, motivated, and competitive. They liked to compete with each other for bonuses. It kept the morale in the organization up. But when the day was over, the managers lived a whole different life. Some of them did drugs and smoked a lot of weed. Some of them got drunk a lot. Some of them chased women. I remember one manager who was very handsome, polite, and friendly. Every time I came in from a territory, he would ask me how my day was, and if I had a bad day he would say, "Oh you'll get it tomorrow!" If I had a good day, he would high-five me and tell me to keep up the good work. I had a crush on him because he was so nice to me. One day in a meeting, we noticed he didn't show up and somebody went to his room to bang on the door and tell him he was late for the morning meeting. He didn't answer the door so they had to get the hotel to open it and they found him dead from an overdose. I couldn't believe it because by looking at him you would never know that he did drugs.

There was this agent that was traveling from San Diego with the crew. He kept the crew motivated but one day he got this really bad cold and kept coughing and sneezing. Then he started running a fever. I had one of the supervisors take him to the hospital. This was around noon, so we called back around 3 o'clock to check on him. They said they were still examining him but to check back in a couple hours. Around seven that evening we called back, and at first they couldn't figure out who we were talking about but then somebody found him and told us that he hadn't made it. I said, "What do you mean he didn't make it? He just went to the hospital 'cause he had a cold and then he went into congestive heart failure?" His heart had stopped and he died about an hour before I called back. I never knew how hard it would be to call someone's mother to tell them that their son had just passed away, but I found out the hard way. That's a cry you never want to hear. It took me three or four days to realize that it wasn't a dream. I had seen him that afternoon and he died just talking like nothing was wrong. He looked like he had a cold and now he was gone. I think these things teach us to appreciate people when they are here because we never know when they will not be.

One of our managers had a pretty nice-sized crew and was on his way to get the payroll for the weekend. While he was out, the other managers in the hotel were running errands and picking up cleaning. When we got back to the hotel, the police were there asking questions...did we know who this manager was? We said yes. One of the policemen said, "Well we just found him in his car deceased. It looked like it was a robbery but they got away before they could take anything. He had a gunshot to his head." At first they said that it was attempted robbery gone bad and then they said it was suicide. Nobody could really figure out what exactly happened but it was strange because nothing was taken and he was a very well-to-do gentleman. He wore nice jewelry, a nice watch, nice chains and rings. The money was gone but there were things in the car—like his cell phone—that hadn't been touched. I have my opinion, and a lot of other people do too, because of the situation of his life and the way things had unfolded. But it was a shame that he had to pass away that way because he was well-loved.

FATHER WHO?

I think I would have been a daddy's girl if I had a father, because for some reason it seems like I always catered to older men. I guess I was looking for a father figure. I remember one time my father did come to visit but I didn't know who he was. I remember him coming into the living room, sitting down and talking to my mother. We had this babysitter that was living with us at the time and I was told the next day that she had left and decided to quit the job. Well, it turns out he came back the next night and climbed up a ladder to her window and took her away. Turns out he got her pregnant and they had a daughter that I met years later. I heard a story about when my mother was young and on her way from school one day, walking past his house. They sparked up a conversation and I guess one thing led to another as she ended up in his house and he and his brother took advantage of her and that's how I got here. I didn't realize the situation until I was twelve years old but I couldn't figure out for the life of me why he never came around. I wanted him to be a part of my life. It bothered me quite a bit because in my travels I would go to New York and look him up but he was always busy. I realized that he was embarrassed about how I was conceived. It made me so angry that every time I saw him and he didn't want to be bothered it would turn into an argument because I let him know how I felt—it was not my fault, so why should I be punished? He had other children from a previous relationship, three boys and a girl. He spent time with them and raised them but never spent any time or did anything for me. I was told that his mother didn't want anything to do with me either because of what he did to my mother and wouldn't help with any support while I was growing up. I always wondered what I did or why I was the only one of his biological children—as a matter of fact, the first one—who he wanted nothing to do with. People say we look just alike so he can't deny me but still he did. That haunted and bothered me for many years, leaving me wondering why everybody had a father except me.

The fact that the men in my life didn't look at me as a daughter made me feel really bad as well, so I had remorse for any man that claimed to be my stepfather but wanted to sleep with me at the same time. I couldn't seem to give any respect to that person. It was funny to me how someone could watch you grow from a little girl into a teenager and be sexually attracted to you. I thought something was wrong with that, but I watched it happen several times with different men in my life so it made me attracted to older men because that's who would always approach me. I'm sure people would say I grew up a little faster than normal but in the situations to which I was accustomed, that's the hand I was dealt. I think it made me the person I am today as far as relationships; I don't accept anything from anybody and they have to be correct to come at me any kind of way. They couldn't just say anything to me—"you're pretty," "you're beautiful," "you have a nice smile and nice body," or "pretty eyes"—because I already knew what I wanted to hear: something I didn't know, like how they really felt about me as a person, what made them want to speak with me, how they felt in my presence, what their motivations were, what really turned them on—those are the things I wanted to know. It's funny how they talked about generational curses and how they somehow seemed to follow you wherever you go because it seems like the same thing happened to my mom. I think these types of men somehow can tell that you've been through some things in your life and you don't like to trust anybody because the first thing they want you to do is trust them. Wow.

I remember this friend of mine when I was younger in New York. They used to always want to come over to my house and play with me. I couldn't figure out why she never wanted to go home, but as I got older it dawned on me that every time she was around her stepfather, she was quiet but when she was around her mother she was happy and positive. Could it be that he was messing with her and she didn't know how to tell anyone? As I look back over the years, I can see that happening. Everything is clear now. She didn't feel good but she never wanted to go home. Life has a way of showing you things if you just pay attention, but I think I realized the true meaning of "when you lay down with dogs you get up with fleas" because even though you try to forget things that have happened to you, somehow they follow you around and you can never shake the bad feelings. Some thoughts keep coming back to you over and over again. Funny that we remember all the bad things but none of the good things, like I can never remember any birthday parties, trips to the beach, playing at the park, or dinners, but I can re-member all the bad things; the hurts, the disappointments, the fear and tears.

SINGING STEPFATHER

When I was twelve years old, I fell down the steps in school and broke my right leg. I had to wear a cast and I couldn't walk for almost a month. I had to be carried and pushed around everywhere I went. One day I was sitting home watching TV and my mother came home from work. As she cooked us dinner, there was a knock on the door and it was this man my mother had met the night before. He looked like Billy Dee Williams—I thought he was so handsome but I had to go upstairs to bed so he picked me up and carried me upstairs. I was in awe because I thought he was a movie star and my mother had said he could sing. As time went on, she got to know him better. He came around more until eventually he just never left. He would go to different places to perform and my mother came up with an idea that we could probably dance for him; he had cut a couple of records and we could be his go-go dancers. She made us these outfits: hot pants and tops with shingles on them. My two cousins and I made up some dance steps and went to the club, acting like we were older than we were. We did our dances and they told us "Okay, it's time to go out on the stage," so we went out and started to dance. I remember either Joe Tex or Wilson Pickett was the star attraction, so we were just the opener. While we were dancing, my stepfather ran out with us and started to sing. It was a very good turn out with people dancing, standing up, clapping, and cheering—he really could sing.

That was probably the most exciting night of my life. I felt like a star and it was all because of him, so I can't say all stepfathers are bad. Though he made one of the best nights of my life memorable, he also made some of my life miserable. He turned out to be an alcoholic and an abuser and I watched him abuse my mom and siblings over the years. For the life of me I couldn't figure out why my mom kept putting up with it. One evening I just couldn't take it anymore and I said something. He slapped me so hard that I thought my head spun around and that's when I decided enough was enough and I was leaving. That's when I left home to pursue a better life for me and my daughter.

LIFELONG FRIEND

One of my dearest friends had issues with her heart. We traveled together for over twenty-five years. Towards the end of her life, her heart started giving her problems. She got to the point where she couldn't breathe and we had to keep taking her to the hospital. Finally she decided that it would be best if she got off the road. She couldn't travel and kept going to the hospital in each city. We kept in touch and talked just like she was still on the road. One day she called me and said she had a hard time the previous night so they rushed her to the hospital and started running tests. I was telling her everything was going to be okay and that I would be praying for her. About a week later she called me and told me that they were taking her to hospice. She said, "Isn't hospice the place you go when you're getting ready to die?" I said, "I'm not sure but I thought so." She said, "Why are they sending me to hospice?" We talked for another thirty minutes or so. The next day I was running errands and I didn't get a chance to talk to her.

When I woke up the next morning and called the hospital to ask why she was in hospice, they couldn't give me any information because I was not a relative. I ended up calling her brother and he told me that she had passed overnight. I couldn't believe that it was so quick. She went to the hospital, then into hospice, and the next day she passed away. It hurt me so bad. I had to go all the way to

Texas for her funeral. I talked to her almost every day for over twenty years. The Lord works in mysterious ways. I sure miss her. We could talk about any and everything. We weren't always the best of friends. It just kind of happened over the years that we began relying on each other for companionship. Companionship turned into friendship. We cried together, laughed together, argued together—but always remained together. Now she's gone and I miss her. It's funny how an acquaintance can become a very dear friend.

I've lost lots of friends and employees over the years from one thing or another. One friend passed away from a heart attack. I watched him drink himself almost to death. Another friend passed away from AIDS. I watched him live recklessly until it caught up with him and took his life. Another friend took a lot of pills and took her own life because she couldn't be with the man she wanted. Life is so short, we should enjoy it while we have it.

SPIRITS

I was a little girl when my stepfather passed away, I remember sitting in bed by myself. I looked at the door and saw almost invisible people pass by. They seemed like they were old people from another time with the old dresses and old military costumes. I could see them looking at me as they passed the door. I could see right through them. I believe spirits linger when they go too soon or very tragically; when they are not quite ready to go. Their spirit might have jumped out too fast and they weren't able to take care of unfinished business. I call them spirits and I do believe that there are a lot of them lingering around, watching over us. We think they're gone but they're not.

ABOUT ATMOSPHERE PRESS

Atmosphere Press is an independent, full-service publisher for excellent books in all genres and for all audiences. Learn more about what we do at atmospherepress.com.

We encourage you to check out some of Atmosphere's latest releases, which are available at Amazon.com and via order from your local bookstore:

The Swing: A Muse's Memoir About Keeping the Artist Alive, by Susan Dennis

Possibilities with Parkinson's: A Fresh Look, by Dr. C

Gaining Altitude - Retirement and Beyond, by Rebecca Milliken

Out and Back: Essays on a Family in Motion, by Elizabeth Templeman

Just Be Honest, by Cindy Yates

You Crazy Vegan: Coming Out as a Vegan Intuitive, by Jessica Ang

Detour: Lose Your Way, Find Your Path, by S. Mariah Rose

To B&B or Not to B&B: Deromanticizing the Dream, by Sue Marko

Convergence: The Interconnection of Extraordinary Experiences, by Barbara Mango and Lynn Miller

Sacred Fool, by Nathan Dean Talamantez

My Place in the Spiral, by Rebecca Beardsall

My Eight Dads, by Mark Kirby

ABOUT THE AUTHOR

Justine Gladden has always thought about putting a lot of things on the wall as far as accomplishments and certificates. After quitting school at an early age, she went back and got her GED. She became a licensed foster parent, then she became a therapeutic foster parent. She has run a home care business for the past eight years. She is a certified notary and is also certified in CPR. Justine is a co-guardian to three special needs children, and has adopted three children. She raised two grown daughters and five beautiful grandchildren. She likes to say that she is "Just working to see how many things I can accomplish before it's all over. I believe the world doesn't owe me anything and I believe when I leave, I will have enjoyed all that life had to offer me."

Made in the USA
Columbia, SC
05 April 2022

58386925R00038